A Scribe's
PARCHMENT

To: Dana Ward
Peace be with you!
22 February 2020

POETRY BY
TIMOTHY J. NEBOYSKEY

ARTWORK BY ALICE MOORE AND TIMOTHY J. NEBOYSKEY

ISBN 978-1-64569-491-5 (paperback)
ISBN 978-1-64569-492-2 (digital)

Christian Faith Publishing, Inc.
832 Park Avenue
Meadville, PA 16335
www.christianfaithpublishing.com

Printed in the United States of America

To my mother,
who bore witness to faith through humility.

ACKNOWLEDGMENTS

Foremost, I want to personally thank all who assisted me with this work in any way. Additionally, I want to impart my gratitude to The Bards of Bird Creek, who ply their versified craft in the Upper Thumb region of Michigan, for their support and inspirational gatherings. I also want to express my heartfelt gratitude to Emory Whaley for her incisive and insightful editing of the manuscript. Finally, I want to humbly convey thanksgiving, for the inexhaustible mysteries of creation…that which surrounds and provisions us…by stating, my hope to never cease admiring all the inherent gifts our temporal home affords.

PREFACE

Whether itinerant or stationary, we are all receivers of Logos, God's word. Within things great and small, abide truths for the sake of one and all. Whether mystical or evident, ethereal or tangible, or perennially fleeting, reality is communicated via providential intent. According to my humble perspective, I have chosen to inscribe some in an attempt to grasp their ultimate purpose. Lest we fail to ponder and speculate upon the unforeseen and neglect gratitude for our daily bread.

Shall we pass through our temporal abode and fail to even remotely consider the great mysteries of life? Shall we wade through the vicissitudes of life and ignore those voices, both still and moving, that speak to our innermost being? For even the greatest scientific and secular theories authored by man inherently require ample amounts of faith to make them coherent. Life is animated by forces unseen and unquantifiable by science alone. It is obvious that if humanity is to successfully grasp the mysteries of life, other disciplines beyond exclusively academic endeavors must be employed as a means for achieving greater understanding. This work is premised upon those fields of endeavor that tend to escape the modern worldview of relevant, scientific classification, and lends itself more readily to classical, western questions; such as: morality, good versus evil, right and wrong, and the nature of our being. May the fields of metaphysics, philosophy, and theology remain ever viable for the sake of keeping western civilization significant and vibrant!

Ad Majorem Dei Gloriam!

A THUMBNAIL SKETCH

Land set apart
seascapes reviving souls
insular varied peoples
Celts Teutons Poles

Landscapes pastoral serene
worn weathered barns
provisioning human cornucopia
elders spinning yarns

A hallowed garden
soil prolific brown
replenished by providence
lavishing farmstead town

O'er hillock dale
grain's intoxicating scent
prophetic breezes wafting
allaying spiritual lament

Thumb's tip jutting
craggy windswept coasts
deep blue enigma
spawning shipwreck ghosts

An Eden ordained
harbors inlets bays
pacifying troubled minds
dunes islets cays

Available for rent
open majestic highways
bygone days discovered
lonely dusty byways

Wayfarers from afar
pilgrims seeking belief
realm of spiritus
believers seeking relief

Progress diverted elsewhere
tradition oriented views
God family country
amply filled pews

Time forgotten earth
flags billowing proudly
blessed by omission
ramblers reveling loudly

Dusky brown adornment
interactive lamps beaming
myriad mesmerized silhouettes
fluorescent orbs gleaming

The Thumb's tip
the Thumb's nail
impressing its impression
impressively without fail

A TOMATO I AM

A tomato I am
or I am not
Is that a question
or an answer?

Despite substantial evidence
to the contrary
challenged by appearance
Nonetheless such sensations persist

The looking glass yields
a spectacle of
plump crimson produce
with attendant stem

Essentially vegetable
my core
succulent hearty fruit
inundated with seed

Such zeitgeist perception
hubris and gravitas
all betray tomato realities—
hence one I am

propelled by hokum
rolling headlong toward
the village common
I became expression

Initially yours truly
intermingled with vegans
but self-preservation
portended tomato-stew

Next I imparted
my newfangled reality
to bohemian relics
who swallowed it verbatim

Nary a one
objected nor exhibited
any scintilla
of doubt

Emboldened—obtaining a
vegetable crate I
planted myself atop
at center common

Paring away platitudes
of my postulation
I enumerated bases
for my recent Metamorphosis

The assembly cheered
while cultural élites
categorically demonstrated delight
for candor un-canned

Most dispatched missives
or crammed notepads
with savory dictums
only now unearthed

Mindful to note
it was they
who witnessed
such phenomena firsthand

With newfound celebrity
senseless anxiety ebbed
bodily calm ascended
I had arrived

Barring skin bruised
by endless pats
of encouragement—courtesy
of kindred spirits

Consummating my delivery
I rolled home
or did I
walk—whatever!

ARITHMETIC

Hate + Hate = Malice

Hate × Hate = Evil

Hate - Love = Gloom

Hate - Hate = Hope

Hate + Love = Human Nature

Hate × Love = Optimism

Love + Love = Loving kindness

Love × Love = Divinity

Love - Hate = Exultation

Love - Love = Despair

BALLOONS

Inflated ego
overladen balloon
stretched capacity
nigh bursting

when poked
immediate eruption
immense transmission
absolute displacement

Deflated ego
supple balloon
reserved capacity
calm air

when poked
leisurely egress
meager response
limited discharge

BATTLEFIELD

Far too often
within my being
a battle rages

Night and day
black or white
good versus evil

Most battles lost
some end better
so it seems?

Lo and behold
all such campaigns
conclude in triumph

Amen 'tis I
who so inject
notions of defeat

For rendered humanity
inclines toward approaching
conflicts with trepidation

From earthly vantage
overall battlefield perspective
is ofttimes unobtainable

Hence significant advances
routinely go unrecorded
nor even recognized

Wanting prominent prospect
victory becomes stalemate
and advantage forfeit

Successes gone uncelebrated
reality becomes clouded
clouds befit reality

As such when
future battles flare
my being trembles

Habitually 'tis I
who so enable
such faulty perception

Via temporal folly
failing to appreciate
elapsed victories drawn

Alas ensuring thus
destined looming battles
dubiety's just deserts

Vainly driven to
make night day
and white gray

Aiding and abetting
all such forces
that flummox battlefields

Future campaigns joined
time and again
despite glorious precedent

Amen 'tis I
who so provoke
dogs of war

Rote injections commandeering
fallible human perspective
mystery camouflaging reality

…rather than humbly
being still—and
concede light's triumph

BEING

To fathom
the esoteric profundity
of life

and soar
upon ethereal thermals
of Spiritus

one must
venture ever deeper
into being

Once there
dread not—Revelation
beckons forth

for therein
experience abounds amid
ineffability untold

for thereby
veils ajar impart
grand design

whereas hearts
tamed by dubiety
seeth not

BLIND MAN

Bestirring about
without demur
noteworthy staff
in tow

He taps this
He taps that
all with purpose
all with care

Observant not to
overlook something
for certain faculties
reflect want

Sonar touch
thus compelled
onus born
safeguarding movement

Lest He
stumble into mishap—
an apparent impediment
of blindness

...still

About He stirs
motivated by Love
or animus
remains unseen

...yet

It matters not
despite keen senses
reality blinds
via paradox

Sight lacking
vision magnified
irreducible itinerary
clear path

Esoteric lodestar
decidedly brilliant
orients bearings
lightening inertia

Bittersweet fruit
outer darkness
inner light
perennial yield

Wanderlust blinded
nary detour
nor trifle
lures He

With relative ease
He stumbles not
bringing to light—
why do I?

BREATH OF LIFE

The wind
it blows
Why?
Nobody knows

Clay inanimate
sparked to life
God concurrent with
man and wife

Consort launching
one to sail
ofttimes so soft
ofttimes a gale

Thee render seed
and occasion rain
thee scurry fauna
and contour grain

I turn away
but thee remain
seeking asylum
with no refrain

CLAY

Clay
I
am

Mold me
Form me
Shape me

In harmony with
ideals originating from
Thy potter's wheel

And if I
diverge from
Thine intended form

then
reshape me
as needed

for as clay
I am reformed
by Thy touch

If I
fail to see—
retouch my eyes

If I
fail to harken—
redo my ears

If I
fail to comprehend—
infuse more light

for as clay
I am destined
for dust

but spiritus
that which animates
this form

How is it
possible that the
spectral vitalizes clay?

…Lo I overextend
Thy clay vessel
lest it break

CONTROL

Lacking control
of emotion

lends to

less command
of reason

liable toward

less mastery
of volition

primed for

less sway
over intention

setting afoot

less reign
over action

making fast

absolute control
of naught

CRUTCHES

Effectively alone
occupying corner stall
perched there—He
clutches gilded crutches
ever so tenaciously

Leaning on supports
conceding their power
superseding His own—
dareth not He
stir without them

Ensconced in belief
that said crutches
possess inherent capacity
to transport Him
far and wide

Satisfied any limitation
ariseth that may
shall be remedied
via the magic
emanating therefrom

Conditioned per environment
disabled by culture
banking on fulcrums
as golden mean
to enhanced being

Deterred by a
worldview that maintains
one is handicapped
minus staunch supports
to sustain them

Yet He remains
oblivious to all
who approach life
flourishing quite admirably
despite scant supports

Bolstered by faith
negotiating daily affairs
sufficiently liberated from
inertia engendered by
technology-laden norms

Occasionally contingencies confer
him blessings—hence
compelled by necessity
realizing latent capacity
freed from bondage

So what doth
lot portend
requisite grace a
leap of faith
or genuine progress?

Or shall He
clutch said crutches
ever tenaciously
and closer still
fettered for aye

never able to
perceive them
as impediments to
not instruments of
enlightened liberation?

DANCING

Whenever we
by volition
defying any dubiety
drawn out indefinitely

Scarcely weighing repercussions
with plausible intent
and nary forethought
dance with Beelzebub

Under macabre moonlight
upon a stage
surreal by nature
embellished with delusion

By God's grace
belatedly we
should pause
and pay heed

Alas when
rhythm and tempo
create such havoc
amid such spectacle

Such being we
shall gambol on
despite one's qualms
despite one's dread

More prudent to
secure oneself tightly
and pray
for reprieve?

Necessarily the folly
shall languish only
when deemed apropos
by Beelzebub

So attune thyself
to another round
because the band
is striking up…

DEDICATION

Oh tender maiden
fair and proper
gracing traditional garb
peering back
with absorbing
awe-stricken eyes
reflecting mine

Conventional bonnet gown
and overcoat
veiling sanctity and
dignifying modesty within
whilst eliciting
genuine esteem
from without

For attending my
inquiring gaze and
deferential perception
endure inherent vestiges
throes of desire
for thy pastoral
mode of living

Humanity predisposes us
to share distortions
of otherness—both
personal and common
reordering one another's
world—refinement serving
inhibition or possibility

Culturally thy
kith and kin
abide by protocols
heretofore deemed obsolete
by fiat exiled
from my world
their comprehension effaced

Yet evermore I
yearn and value
their worth still
whilst sifting about
occasionally lighting upon
such virtues amid
conditions most familiar

Alas to cherish
our fleeting encounter
since thy cameo
pleasing and innocent
featuring attentive orbs
imbues me with
faith and hope

A hope someday
my world may
progress toward thine
and ultimately thee
shall preserve those
timeless traditions that
strayed from mine

Dedicated to Amish traditions, Cass City, Michigan on 17 November 1999. Rededicated on 02 October 2006, for Nickel Mines, Pennsylvania.

DEEDS

Wherever I go
they follow

The past
scripted montage
occasionally vivid
occasionally not

My mind
cannot escape
my memory
cannot erase

On odysseys
they trail
on knees
they harry

In dreams
they prevail
But how?
And why?

A delivery
improbable
a redo
impossible

...so whither
I go—
What must
I do?

Cherish
good memories
learn
from reflection

For
tomorrow dawns
rendering hope
delivering renewal

DIVINE CHANCE

Accorded a chance
cracking open
Heaven's veil
I peered inside

Populated with multitudes
a specific search
seemed fruitless
even quixotic

Yet temporal ambition
impelled me forth
to progress beyond
inherently truncated vistas

So I commenced
my quest…

Some were familiar
most were not
I greeted
family friends neighbors

After reciprocal pleasantries
I delved further
endeavoring to
conciliate latent curiosity

Reclining at table
partaking of fruits
that the
Heavenly feast affords

A familiar face
A perceptive chap
A protagonist
of modernity

A humanist
who championed
man's
natural virtues

Savoring eternal salvation
ensconced in place
consummately jubilant
set at peace

An individual who
of old swimmingly
sowed skepticism toward
such a place

Where quite ironically
its reality
he now prizes
with pure delight

Evidently he
evolved over time
Metamorphosis occasioned by
conversion of soul

For His work
cast doubt upon
universal intelligence
a Divine purpose

'Via natural selection
we all morphed
from primordial soup
perchance by fortuity'

Via innumerous mutations
occurring at random
in concurrence with
highly improbable probability

Yet as fate
would have it
graciously this soul
was transformed anew

And His countenance
illuminating unmitigated triumph
providing evidence
that temporal endeavors

When chance reigned
have been eclipsed
by Providence
and thankfully so!

ENQUIRY

What
do we know
and how
is it known?

Clearly we've
garnered insight
from yore
'till now

Exempli Gratia
we abide
and soon
Azrael arrives

Besides
with certainty
most exists
beyond our scope

So—what
doth this bare
and whence
doth it lead?

Shall we
go mad searching
in continuous pursuit
of what?

We know enough
to know
that good
surmounts evil

And denying good
abets evil—
lest we forget
what we know

§ II

Man
seeking endlessly
for accounts
to all

finds
endless seeking
to account
for all

Anxiety and
pride combine
forming an
unsettled modality

Man
seeking endlessly
for truth
to all

finds
endless truth
to seek
for all

Content and
humility combine
forming a
settled modality

FAITH

Damn the one
who governs night
when darkness cons
mind and sight

Woe to those
believing what might
with passing thoughts
Flee or fight?

Seek staunch faith
to counter fright
hail each dawn
heralding new light

FREEDOM AND BLOOD

Wolność
i krew

freedom
and blood

life
and death

heart
and soul

winter
and spring

night
and day

good
and evil

hard
and soft

white
and red

Laws
of nature

all
are interwoven

all
are inseparable

One
cannot exist

without
the other

and
when some

insist
on believing

that
these realities

can
exist independently

then
they should

ultimately
prepare for

the
inevitable surrender

of
their freedom

and
their blood

FRESH AIR

Above nebulous vault
below furling froth
within throbbing heart

My plea—impart
for now
reception is prime

Loch-laden breeze
fresh from traversal
refined naturally

Zephyr's breath
warm and moist
resuscitates being

being—

Liable to
outer clatter
and inner clutter

Prevailing wind-stream
sweeps one direction
my course another

Which way delivers?

Azure loft
aqua abyss
emerald vantage

Golden strands
tracing bounds
fathomable and non

Natural wonder
'fore us arrayed
betray yore secrets

Lucid above
obscure below—
A clue perchance?

With ear attuned
soul rendered agape
said being awaits…

Beyond the horizon
time and space
apparent mysteries

Universal revelation
conceivably infinite
infinitely conceivable

Eden abides
sow thy hope
tend thy dreams

From all fruit
within each morsel
miracles abound

Marvel consciously
savor earnestly
life's confirmation

Manistee, Michigan, 06 October 2007.

GREED

Overheard
a man
disparaging his benefactors
they savor all
whilst he naught

Dashingly
hurtling homeward
in swank setup
poshly provisioned
simmering over debt—

Notably
tony transport
distinct domicile
hallowed Hog
ostentatious odysseys

…and
so on

Relenting
to red
beyond the tracks
within marginal parts
a man loomed

Destitution
duly displayed
tattered togs
donned daily
appearances aroused amity

Bread
lunch-bag leavings
something to sustain
another dawn
palms petitioned pacifically

Perturbed
rancor rising
preferring progress
over privation
he hastened off

Snarling
'Sordid sight
is he
obtain a job
like me'

Oblivious
cruising along
toward agreeable abode
attentive mate
and rich repast

Unbound
easy chair recumbent
elixir in tow
hearth's milieu
warm and exclusive

Overheard
another encore
right on cue
shopworn litany
damnation of benefactors

...lo
lest ye
posit fault without
ye must foremost
amend fault within

HATE

Harrowed heart
menacing memory
caustic core
embedded egotism

Corroded conscience
bedeviled being
derelict disposition
wanton will

Nefarious nature
petulant purpose
punitive posture
malignant moil

Sinister seed
fetid fruit
desolate darnel
investing iniquity

Ardent antipathy
specious sowing
ravenous reaping
perennial perdition

Deliberate descent
ingrained infirmity
spiritual suicide—
Absolved animus?

Forgiveness
and reconciliation

Rendered and requested
remedial regimen
bathes being
of spiritual Sheol

HERE AND THERE

Here
there
and everywhere

Why
am I *here*
and not *there*?

As
many assert—I
could be there

Given
expectations linked to
uprooting and relocation

But
with roots
embedded there

What
fruit shall stem
from it?

Shall my taproot
burrow deep
and adaptation ensue?

Shall I unearth
true bliss
or even serenity?

Shall this passage
bear harvests of
hearth and kin?

Shall I grow
in wisdom
and integrity?

Or
shall I after
an indefinite stay

determine
when there
ultimately becomes here

that
I am there
and not here

for
specific purposes
hitherto purposely unspecified?

§ II

With
grandiose odysseys a
departure point befalls

when
one is more
there than here

But
what constitutes
here and there?

Must
one delve into
time and space

can
energy and motion
be effectively exempted

can
measures of philosophy
and science help?

Do
compulsory stimuli
frame this riddle

or
can transformation occur
via another way?

Shall
body mind and
soul be renewed

by
being there
and not here?

Moreover
being there
ensures another paradox

since
biding afar annuls
any arrival here

Hence
is it crucial
to venture there

in
order to
arrive?

For
is it not
merely with access

to
truth's threshold that
one actually arrives?

HIKE

Into wilderness
a hike
trailing solitude
instead naturally
gleaned inspiration

Bound for
forest primeval
engaging nature
seeking nexus
as intended

Post toil
and span
on trail
a man
exuding creation

Nay earth
nor humanity
represented he
flittering along
with ease

Via zeal
face aglow
eyes ablaze
boding prevalence
of spirit

Dispensing protocol
avoiding judgment
without delay
pursuing instead
matters deep

Blazing straight
a path
my soul
rend open
rendered anew

Tacit parlance
expressed he
cherishing our
fated meet
and life

Smiling cordially
nodding humbly
tipping cap
turning about
destined yon

Upright disabled
weighing variables—
to follow
and detect
his impetus?

Reclining gradually
verity mused
daylight passed
moments indistinct
from eternity

Although encounters
may embody
time shards
their effects
abide forever

Our confluence
suspending physics
shedding mortality
accorded us
spiritual nexus

Pensive thoughts
mystical milieu
…humanity returned
bearings set
for home

I AM...

I am...
a human spirit
and spiritually human

an orthodox Catholic
qualified via sin
faithful by grace

an American Pole
flavored with Norman
and European seasoning

a humble traditionalist
consciously vigilant
but curious intellectually

a grateful worker
working gratefully
for truth

...I am created
conceived thus
I am

hence
I am
because I am

likewise
I am not
...I am

IDLENESS

Life
purpose found wanting

all
available and abundant

plenitude
prepared and prodigal

pleasure
predominant and proliferous

sacrifice
snubbed and slighted

everything
to live for

nothing
to die for

...falling
into the stream

in
no particular fashion

for
no specific reason

he
joined the current

driftwood
carried by flow

landing
directed by dynamics

...he
was found wanting

nobility
will means conditioning

all
essential and integral

to
evade the stream

and
withstand the current

INHERITANCE

Temporally

Can one live
down the block
and be
God's neighbor?

Across the way
beyond mortal manors
nigh spacious squares
abides Almighty's abode

Nearby a crown
celestial raiment
a supernal scepter
the royal seat

A capstone
ritually set
denying the enemy
favorable light

Lo and behold
for Zion prevails
steadfast solemnity
sublime pre-eminence

Yet prophetically can
a community comprising
comprehensively diverse worldviews
be shared peacefully?

Children
obdurately wrangling
over Paternal
inheritance

Not infrequently appointed
universal treasure
a precious *possession*
quartered to share

Its appraised value
beyond human calculation
its veritable worth
beyond human comprehension

Concisely its value
transcends all
monetary and
temporal holdings combined

Hence its worth
ensures heirs
both triumph
and tribulation

Kinship with it
naturally drives
many mad—despite
exaltation and ecstasy

Such hallowed holdings
adorned for ages
cannot but be
venerated

Disregarding it abets
ambiguity—denying it
authorizes doubt—debasing
it actuates peril

For select seasons
some have safeguarded
their heritage—only
to lose it

Yet dwelleth
nary temporal power
nor mortal wisdom
to secure it

Absent divine intervention
or Providence
is possession
mere delusion?

Do those with
title or claim
of inheritance *ever*
actually own it

Or are they
custodial heirs until
ownership is established
ad infinitum?

JOHN PAUL II

Duly gleaned patronymic
divined by empyrean
or humble servant?
Commissioned to pasture
our Shepherd's fold

John
beloved by Jesus
guardian of Mary
scribe ever incisive
For God so
loved the world... (John 3:16)

Paul
by Jesus appointed
to sow tidings
of everlasting life
Where O death
is thy victory? (I Corinthians 15:55)

II
a sanctioned continuum
inheriting select gifts
petrifying them twofold
an augmentation of
magnitude and caliber

in consummation
via divine intent
and humble service
all so graced
Be not afraid! (Matthew 28:10)

LUMINESCENCE

Temporally

Paris is the
City of Light
because we dwelleth
in darkness

Lamps liberally distributed
and aptly arrayed
yet shadows persist
sheltering earthly iniquity

Many a detour
down side street
or hidden square
for indulgence incognito

Unto humanity
a beacon
orienting imperiled vessels
moths to flame

…whereas eternally

Jerusalem is the
City of Light
which by its
very nature

Reveals to mankind
all known iniquities
that dwelleth
upon earth

And by fate
shall doom darkness
casting it off
into oblivion

Unto the world
a beacon
orienting all vessels
dusk into dawn

MODERNITY

An open letter
to God,
Let us commence
by conveying
our indebtedness for
Your magnanimous deeds
and by acknowledging
that You are
a good deity

but Your plan
has gone awry
and is passé
for example
the Good Book
humanity culture
and mother earth
are found wanting
and in disarray

besides we have
evolved into more
enlightened beings and
can now administer
our own affairs
moreover human ideas
have progressed so
to permit us
explanations for *all*

currently we believe
man is
a perfectible being
one no longer
requiring Your attentive
paternalism—rather than
a flawed creature
that relies upon
Your grace

for science now
preoccupies our endeavors
confidence and
articles of faith
embodying our hope
it is
the vehicle via
which we facilitate
man's evolutionary progress

despite the fact
our nouveau religion
springs from probability
and on average
medial probability
at best
we nonetheless believe
because it's tangible
whereas You're not

on another issue
regarding the topic
of social cadence
Buddha and Confucius
are popular while
You are not
Judaism and Christianity
have been superseded
by eastern mysticism

can You refute
the deduction
that meditation
perennial veritable rebirth
and cosmic awareness
are just
more tolerable than
sacrifice fasting
and prayer?

We reiterate our
indebtedness for all
Your benevolence—but
destiny is now
ours to manage
…oh and God
don't summon us
we'll summon you
…if need be.

Postscript

For within the
constitution of modernity
abides the conceit
that 'God although
an exceedingly brilliant
and magnanimous deity'
nevertheless 'He overlooked
a few details'
Quite the contrary

nay verily the
oversight dwells within
human arrogance and
its twin: ignorance
for who has
failed to calculate
the equation properly:
the temporal mind
or its Creator?

MR. SPIDER

Okay Mr. Spider
I'll cut a
deal with you

I pledge to
not rend asunder
your fibrous labyrinth

Meticulously spun
in the niche
of my porch

Where post
meets stairway
and weds banister

If you
consent to communicate
with me?

Render your sense
of Luna
luminous on high

The elements
that fitfully beset
your web

And your verdict
on life—from
an arachnid's vantage

Bemoanfully
my entreaty is
fanciful at best

Consequently I am
compelled to inject
by proxy

Credible responses
to this inquiry
for you

Hmmm after
earnest contemplation—Athena
intimates you are

Essentially utilitarian
in that subsistence
preoccupies your day

Let alone
that you are
incapable of pondering

The cosmos
assailing elements
nor existence

Yet via inference
a resplendent moon
eases your craft

Permitting a
commanding view
of prey entangled

Conversely brilliant luminosity
could restrict dining
by betraying meshwork

Hence you must
retain mixed sensibilities
toward such wonder

And whenever
atmospheric forces
harry sinewy abodes

What possibilities exist
beyond holding out
for better conditions?

As for the
inexhaustible and insoluble
riddles of life

I surmise despite
endless hours spent
in acute anticipation

You are rapt
with much more
pertinent matters

To squander precious
time pondering imponderables
as yours truly

NEW AGE

Lo for a
new age dawns
smitten with heterodoxy
masquerading as novelty

When myriad
solicit intuition
to decrypt
their derivation

And masses
seek shamans
to divine
their destiny

And many
spurn clergy
who determine
their disposition

For with
proper footing
past and future
matter less

Yet less matters
especially footing
past and future
hence become venerable

'Tis the season
to forego tradition
and indulge progress
whither it leads.

§ II

Age of Aquarius
mythical revival
existential bathos
consciousness eclipses wisdom

Fish enter water
spawning nigh Atlantis
sign of times
legend or history?

Recycled thought ascendant
sentiment supersedes fact
synchronized relativity
tempus fugit

Insight overshadows doctrine
altered spirits abound
experience outshines ritual
conform or wilt

Cosmic cavalcade
energy for worship
elude great light
revealing natural law

Personal truths prevail
minds master matter
as constellations align
all become god

NURSERY

Across infinity
a trumpet
heralded forth

'An upturn
in recalls
shall commence posthaste'

ranging from
ordinary to novel
chronic and acute

entrusted commands
angels of death
reap the harvest

...of late Paradise
set to overflowing
with nay-born souls

recent arrivals
a multitude
generate reaction

hence
such conditions
ordain absolute measures

as such
mortal pride
importunes elect tenders

patrons
to mind
pure souls

…bittersweet yield
discordant with
the Master plan

the harvest
is rich but
laborers are few

better to
retain reaping
within Heaven's sway

with deceit sown
effectively and prodigiously
given such

can God
but so choose
not to act

in accordance
with His plan
within His world?

ORCHARDS

The abundant life
veritable bounty lavished
a man blessed
jubilant via dominion
over an eminently
fruitful orchard

Bearing specimens
of superb quality
a genuine regale
for said man
myriad feathered birds
and other creatures

Earth hallowed by
Providential elements
replenished rich soil
a nurturing medley
enabling the basis
for succulent cornucopia

Spoiled by bliss
insipid from contentment
compelled by mystery
to seek
analogous orchards
for other fruit

Fancying himself liberated
harboring reservations toward
perceived confines
and native roots
off wandered man
for discovery

Rambling a spell
traversing both
mead and woodland
propelled by desire
to delight in
truly unique fruit

Submitting to necessities
naturally obliging
respite and sustenance
his being beseeched
sabbath within a
markedly alluring grove

Availing exotic fruit
seductive and luscious
the orchard appealed
to senses—now
in dire need
of replenishment

The tenders
sunny and hospitable
introducing him to
expressly succulent strains
soliciting unbridled participation
to mollycoddle appetite

Once sated
invariably corporeal conditions
oriented him toward
a remote spot—
respite where grove
melds wilderness

Swiftly as a
summer tide tempest
Morpheus overcame him—
yet serene slumber
proved elusive
dooming any revival

His bed
uneven and hard
preventing basic relaxation
his nerves
taut and frayed
intensified by fructose

His stomach
knotted and churning
unable to assimilate
with routine efficiency
fruit—so ambrosial
and profoundly exotic

his mind
hijacked by imagination
dissonant via novelty
denied familiar surroundings
it in turn
denied him tranquility

All the while
infernal beasts
sly and uncanny
staged nigh—fervid
to appease voracity
with select fruit

Lacking proper defenses
dread in ascent
engorging to excess
hideous sounds wafting
abject gloom attending
paranoia's primeval feast

With dawn
ensued retreat of
beast and fear
in spite of
blinding sunlight—repose
finally delivered him

His dreamscape
melodrama beset
by a montage
of orchard home
bearing fruit of
sustenance and life

Availing all provisions
of abundant life
so readily
such that complacency
and idle curiosity
become possible

Upon rising
refreshed and revived
despite dusk descending
following inner light
he set off
for home

PASSION

For it
had to be
the most inhuman
execution throughout history
of set purpose
absolving all
mortal beings from
knowing or experiencing
greater redemptive suffering

And for purposes
of impelling those
so initiated
to plunge precipitously
upon knees
in reverence praise
and devotion
Inspiring them to
follow His way

And to
countermand sinful ways
substantiating truth He
prepared the Way
a set path—
O polestar divine
orienting man's bearings
away from darkness
and toward light

And to
render redemption for
the ever-burgeoning multitude
of sins—both
seen and unseen
irrespective of
type nor degree
perpetrated across
the temporal spectrum

And to
crown Atonement
securing an ever-closer
relationship betwixt
Creator and created
as exemplified via
humble sacrifice—that
no one has
loved us more

And to
unbar the gate
to our
eternal pasture
as both
Lamb and Shepherd
heralding the era
when His sheep
shall graze blissfully

And to…

PER YOUTHFUL EYES

Per youthful eyes
a bucolic merry-go-round
is instead
a dashing carrousel

Exuberant frolic is
not remedial respite
but a
wonted escapade

Stable dung is
nary vile refuse
but the catalyst
for coltish bantering

Blissful laughter
idiom of play
expressed freely
imparted hospitably

Words are unmeasured
thoughts direct
reality untested
milieu abiding amusement

The world—but
a playground bedecked
with sundry gizmos
determined by elders

Life is
but a game
seasoned by levity
punctuated with awe

Per youthful eyes
hope accommodates joy
being affords promise
dreams are possible

PINUS STROBUS

Oh
my dear tree
I am
enamored with you
again

Erewhile
I was implacably
loyal to
a propensity for
symmetry

Naturally
this predisposed me
toward your
cousin Pinus resinosa
provisionally

Verily
I grant thee
my dalliance
was inordinately long
regrettably

But
now I'm cognizant
that symmetry
can also propagate
languor

For
I've come to
eminently revere
and conclusively favor
irregularity

Behold
your profile is
disproportionate—betraying
dignity unaffected by
uniformity

This
one may deduce
properly befits
more than not
individuality

Do
your variations reveal
a free-spirit
resisting compulsion to
conform?

Whereby
in an increasingly
homogenous world
conformity is oft-labelled
nonconformity

For
in comparison to
other pines
your irregularity is
liberating

And
in its most
accurate import
your unfettered semblance
inspires

Me
to be more
insistent of
and bound to
authenticity

Incidentally
in fitting summation
Michigan evokes
wisdom by honoring
you

PORTALS

As one
portal closes
others open

post-closure
seek ye
another

initially
search
beyond self

if found
render praise
render thanks

if not
render praise
render thanks

...for

thy portal
beckons ye
within

PREVAILING WIND

Am I

Solid
stanch
relevant

open
resilient
consoling?

Or

Am
I akin
to wind?

Capricious
restive
abrupt

normal
cogent
prevalent?

Life
inhaled exhaled
fresh stale

felt
never seen
barring effects

overheard
tussling creation
occasionally boisterous

presence
known unknown
virtually incognito

posit
hither thither
or whither?

Meeting
fixed unfixed
objects

coming
and going
randomly swiftly

…gone
whither to
and why?

Gone
like the
wind

…better

to
be sown
by wind

than
to futilely
chase it

PROVERBS

I

Mind over matter
...yet there shall
come a day

when matter
shall not
mind the mind

and in this
matter the mind
shall not matter

II

If one is
unwilling to sacrifice
mercifully for their
mode of living

then one's
mode of living
will be mercifully
sacrificed

...if most are
certainly unwilling to
die for their
way of life

then their
way of life
will most certainly
die

III

If you can't
trust a man
in small things

then you can't
trust him
in great things

and

if you can't
trust a man
in small things

then you can't
trust him
in anything

IV

Never
have so many
savored so much

yet
appreciate so much
so very little

…so
with such ingratitude
what shall ensue?

Duly
much shall be
sown amongst many

who
indelibly appreciate it
so much more

V

Sunlight
sans Sol

rain
minus clouds

truth
without reality

…even
more so—

law
absent morality

VI

Ego
equals
sensitivity

greater egos
equal
greater sensitivity

lesser egos
equal
lesser sensitivity

…well-being
parallels
defense

greater insecurity
demands d'fence
be grandiose

greater security
destines d'fence
be modest

VII

By
hate
blinded

teetering marionettes
on thy adversary's
strand

by
love
edified

perpetual clay
on thy Potter's
wheel

VIII

If ye
habitually with earnest
serve others

via reciprocity
ye shall
be served

if ye
habitually with earnest
serve thyself

via reciprocity
ye shall not
be served

...by serving others
one ultimately
serves thyself

by serving thyself
one ultimately
denies thyself others

IX

Life is
a carousel

immutably beset
on round

seek not
it's entertainment

instead decipher
passing vistas

X

I am
therefore
I think

we live
hence
we breathe

I believe
therefore
I hope

we endeavor
hence
we dream

…I'm free
therefore
I obey

PURPOSE

If there is
purpose
in everything

then
everything has
purpose

...and if
everything has
purpose

then the
purpose
of everything

was purposed
to be
purposeful

REAPING

A reaper sowed
tangible seed
favorable conditions
produced bounty
mundane feasting
spiritual fasting

another reaper sowed
supernal seed
favorable conditions
produced bounty
mundane fasting
spiritual feasting

the Reaper sows
all seed
divine Providence
favors bounty
solemn feasting
deliberate fasting

RECIPROCITY

Give ye benevolently
all the more
ye shall receive

in due accord
thy endeavors shall
render thee joy

…whereas

horde ye faithfully
all the more
ye shall covet

in due accord
thy endeavors shall
deny thee joy

SIN

Behold the sun
ye turn away
a shadow forms
business is conducted

endemic to shade
privacy is perceived
folly gains supremacy
darkness humors obscurity

yet all around
the daystar reigns
all is seen
bathed in light

...and the shadow?
Nothing but delusion
reality ignored tenfold
favoring relative darkness

SOUL

Whilst engaging
life's great mystery
whilst negotiating
life's epic trial

with respect
consider mortal perspective
with wisdom
regard relevant insight

hence glean
knowledge from fact
and seek
truth beyond time

via truth
ye shall fortify
via untruth
all shall fail

for strength
draw from within
for wisdom
sift from without

since much
is provided within
and much
is redundant without

with dignity
doubt thy world
with diligence
tend thy being

…thus sow
the Holy Spirit
and reap
thy inherent soul

for therein
integrity rewards endeavor
and thereby
love renders mercy

SOUP

Whenever water is
admixed with soup
stretching its capacity
of set purpose
to sustain more—
without fail this
shall be fulfilled

with unabated dilution
manifold stomachs
can be appeased
as evinced by
myriad sidetracked vessels
emptied of contents
by hungry souls

but what of
the resulting concoction
for all who
partake of it
shall their experience
purvey more
or less nutrition?

SPRING

Boreas exhaled vigorously
my progress repelled
several bellicose blasts
compelled involuntary retreat

Everywhere the landscape
naked barren
its solitary yield
drab withered degradation

Even a snowscape
ivory and pure
winter's suitable splendor
elevates select spirits

Yet as lot
opted to stage
slate gray firmament
attended torpid earth

Despondent
staggering hearth bound
succumbing to hibernation
melancholy overcame me

...eventually I awoke
to spirited melodies
songbirds singing festally
heralding another dawn

Aroused curiosity
impelled me outside
a crisp morn
with blinding brilliance

All around
vernal earth
bearing copious fruit
spring's verdant marvel

Notus' gentle breath
rippled burgeoning greenery
dormant spirit refreshed
every inhalation savored

Revived—roving about
animated by awe
ubiquitous life throbbing
…ultimately life prevails

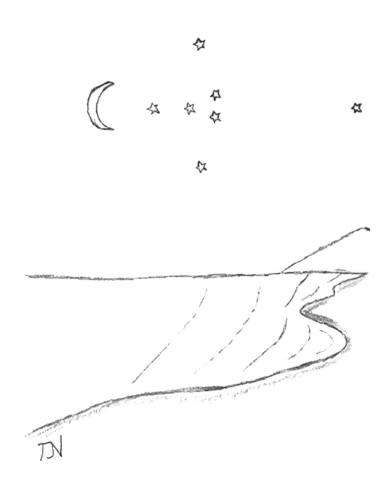

STELLAR SILENCE?

Winter solstice
pervasive frigidity
pastoral snowscape
remarkable calm
resonant silence

eminently above
stellar firmament
whispering softly
traversing space
illustrating time

twinkling acclamation
'Yes indeed
via wonder
we adore
Him too!'

Upper Peninsula, Michigan, 14 September 2006

STORY?

Who shall tell
our story?

Our beloved brood
and extended kin
or those maligning
our mere being?

Our cherished friends
and steadfast confidants
or those profiting
from our defects?

Our fellow citizens
and religious affiliates
or those deeming
us as foes?

Our venerable traditions
and unifying ideals
or those seeking
our ideal schism?

Who shall tell
our story?

Be fruitful
and multiply
and thy seed
shall narrate perennially

Eat drink
and be merry
and others shall
generate fruitful alternatives

THE BIRDS OF BARD CREEK

A chittering covey
flocking frequently
cheering Bard Creek

beneficent banks
availing ambrosia
morsels for many

nourishing naturally
seed for subjectivity
posterity's pulp

a fruitful gathering
or gathering fruit
literally a feast

THE BRIDGE

The Bridge
suspended betwixt
empyrean and orb
bestridden both
embracing each
with thresholds
at opposite ends

This link
connected to both
bridging the breach
for ages parted
an abyss overcome
a span made
to foster communication

A causeway
to save time
and surmount space
facilitating access
to and fro
by way of
all hope passes

A bridge
melding disparate realms
undergirding elevated harmony
becoming the manifested
conduit of peace
enabling augmented
and improved admission

This bridge
servant of all
who seek to
amend their spirit
and overcome conditions
to soar over
indelibly perfect spans

This bridge
the essential link
comprised of empyrean
comprised of orb
a span betwixt
point of nexus
arbiter for both

This bridge
the ultimate gift
for all time
a new creation
specifically made
to reconcile both
by being both

A bridge
skeleton and flesh
evident and mystery
congruent yet transcending
requiring maintenance and
replacement—occasionally collapsing
not the above

Made to cross
hate with love
sin with redemption
death with life
time with eternity
all with truth—
Heaven and earth

THE ONLY VOICES...

At home
the only voices
domesticating the landscape
are bird's

One day
while steering homeward
I beheld
cherubic lasses

Embracing cats
dogs everyone
with unconditional love
by unqualified means

Laying bare
pumpkin-sized hearts
and deportment
as yet unrefined

By social expediency
and cultural norms
girls transform
into women

But what should
I expect—for
is this not
their nature?

As for birds
their flittering graces
and avian antics
bespeak freedom

Melodious calls
animation in abundance
provide endless
hours of fascination

but they don't
seek human intimacy
nor fraternity—such
inheritance they lack

Any attempt to
make their acquaintance
naturally triggers
self-preservation

Whereby their persons
and offspring instinctively
are placed before
soliciting human association

But what should
I expect—for
is this not
their nature?

TOLERANCE

I practiced tolerance
in deference to
novelty and fashion

via social cadence
short-term gains
became common

yet over time
problems erased progress
by tolerating everything

as events evolved
social cadence became
submission to marginalization

…whereas when

I practiced love
it was deemed
passé and deficient

via social cadence
short-term gains
were illusory

yet over time
progress erased problems
by tolerating nothing

as events evolved
social cadence became
marginalized via love

TREE OF LIFE

Upright above
an emerald mead
it abides there
eminently flourishing—the
tree of life

Systemic self-perpetuating perfection
vitality slumber revival
provisions for posterity
all in accordance
with natural law

Mature distinguished substantial
nature's floral masterpiece
courtesy of Providence
a bard's inspiration
a child's sanctuary

Lush purposeful foliage
sustaining life
by wondrous means
despite contrary claims
lifeblood via Sol

From vernal buds
hope springs eternal
creation's timepiece
shade for passerby
mulch for posterity

Beneath the surface
beyond one's view
roots burrow deep
and afar
anchoring the system

Co-opting the netherworld
for vital resources
subterranean agents acting
to secure sustenance
and enrich life

bearing copious fruit
seasoned for perfection
arrayed brilliantly
to facilitate acquisition
and nurture humanity

morsels of mystery
replete with nectar
inducing external participation
but what of
the mysteries within?

Ample mysteries readily
available for apprehension
yet true revelation
entails greater effort
(and grace)

And prophetic wisdom
to pursue morsels
arduous to gather
and exist beyond
one's immediate grasp

TRUTH

Undivided undefiled unrefined
absolute infinite eternal
independent immutable universal

Power to humble
power to exalt
authority via reality

Clay vessels decay
empires always decline
truth never fails

Black or white
Black and blue
but never gray

Sovereign in nature
denial is fruitless
denial is mortal

Amen thy being
nary requires temporal
assent nor dissent

Good springs forth
more from use
than from not

Certainly never passé
certainly never void
in fashion forever

Whether on knees
or standing tall
genuine freedom assured

Indelibly a danger
for the oppressed
and their oppressors

Thee incite Mars
thee incite Venus
Thee art life

Behold yon mount
behold yon cloud
behold the Word

…what becomes self-evident
by denying truth
one denies reality

By denying reality
one provokes nature
by provoking truth

One provokes truth
in that aberration
righteously becomes reality

Realizing aberrant reality
depravity reigns supreme
calamity equals justice

And when justice
graciously effects prostration
one is liberated

And with liberation
ultimately one can
accept truth's reality

UNQUENCHABLE FIRE

O tender maiden
thee hath ignited
an unquenchable fire
ablaze me orbs
crackle and sparkle
in result

Whose dominion
and mystery
as with
the burning bush
render me unto
ineffable awe

I remove
my sandals
as if
on holy ground
venerating the presence
of divine intent

And to defile
thy nature
is to sully
the express purpose
of our Creator's
venerable design

VINES

Souls animate humanity

Humanity gleans knowledge
knowledge refines patience
patience burnishes wisdom
wisdom befits insight
insight abets virtue
virtue ennobles strength
strength adorns faith
faith arrays love
love fulfils hope
hope enriches passion
passion nurtures courage
courage ensures justice
justice obeys truth
truth attends holiness
holiness delivers enlightenment
enlightenment exalts sacrifice
sacrifice enables suffering
suffering reaps mercy
mercy illumines divinity
divinity sanctifies crucifixion
crucifixion redeems souls

VOICES?

I heard a
voice cry out
from yon wood

believing my senses
were mistaken—silent
there I stood

at first it
was low and
ever so shrill

but today I
hear it louder
and clearer still

for 'twas
long ago
and far away

whilst on me
way for what
I cannot say?

Yet this matters
not—because I
heard it still

piercing the solitude
and nullifying
a twilight chill

I paused for
a spell to
clear my head

and permit the
harbinger to rehash
what he said

he echoed his
tidings in a
calm clear tone

whilst his words
did admonish—rechilling
every last bone

recalling what has
been and what
is now

he then cited
the future which
furrowed my brow

'With past as
teacher and present
as guide

our fate is
bleak lest we
stem our pride

for we've tools
and gifts to
secure brighter days

if only we
resolve to
mend our ways?!'

...But I scurried
along—concerned solely
with creating space

betwixt me and
him so I
quickened my pace

providing scant attention
to words
that whilst blue

were certainly then
and today
are true

...yet anxious genes
assumed primacy and
I took flight

but now minus
fear—I know
he was right

WINDOWS

Two eyes
one Soul

chaos circling
calm within

via floral-land
loom keys

rendered sparks
pore therein

…beyond—the
great chasm

free will
versus heed

…occasioning some
to query

Who is
in control

flesh or
the Soul?

WOLVES

When sheep
become their own
shepherds

A field day
wolves
shall have

Wholeheartedly clad
in the fleece
of self-delusion

Insatiably feasting upon
the flesh
of egoism

…beyond the fold
predation continues unabated
until dawn

Luminary on high
the Shepherd returns
redeeming His flock

WORDS

What
constitutes
a word?

Are they essentially
tangible incorporeal or
mental in nature?

Aha! Mortals may
posit they are
tangible—of course

as evinced by
dark characters
patronizing light backgrounds

...do they
waft about in
time and space

subjected to
naught nor
no one

a continuum
spinning yarns round
laws of physics

or does their
composition comport verbatim
with established laws?

Do certain characters
that comprise words
import optimal qualities?

Are they genuinely
ways and means
to convey ideas

or simply stated
are they terms
of ideal communication?

Are words
telltale vestiges
of being

transformed
from spirit
into corporeality

streams of thought
converting subjectivity
quite objectively

soul to soul
human to human
for all ages?

What of
the oral
word?

Do they become
perceptible only on
brisk wintry morns?

From material paucity
can one infer
a subordinate clause

or does their
dearth of substance
connote something more?

Said word bound
nary by paper
nor any text

continuously at large
expressly milling about
cosmic realms

to manifest wherever
whenever and within
whomever it pleases

to traverse the
universal mind seeking
a receptive host

when found
to augment intellects
of sufficient suitability

...oh my word
with all this
ruminating on wordplay

my mind
has literally
succumbed to overload

ABOUT THE AUTHOR

Timothy J. Neboyskey is a veteran of the US Army. Later, he received degrees from St. Mary's College (Michigan) and the University of Michigan. Currently a resident of Charlevoix, Michigan, he is active in his parish (St. Mary) and with the Knights of Columbus.

.

CPSIA information can be obtained
at www.ICGtesting.com
Printed in the USA
FFHW021813101019
55440595-61249FF

9 781645 694915